Investigating landscapes

Caroline Clissold

www.heinemann.co.uk/library

Visit our website to find out more information about **Heinemann Library** books.

To order:
- ☎ Phone 44 (0) 1865 888066
- 📄 Send a fax to 44 (0) 1865 314091
- 💻 Visit the Heinemann Bookshop at www.heinemann.co.uk/library to browse our catalogue and order online.

First published in Great Britain by Heinemann Library, Halley Court, Jordan Hill, Oxford OX2 8EJ, part of Harcourt Education. Heinemann is a registered trademark of Harcourt Education Ltd.

Editorial: Vicki Yates
Design: Dave Poole and Tokay Interactive Limited (www.tokay.co.uk)
Illustrations: Geoff Ward and International Mapping (www.internationalmapping.com)
Picture Research: Hannah Taylor
Production: Duncan Gilbert

Originated by Repro Multi Warna
Printed in China by WKT Company Limited

10 digit ISBN: 0 431 03252 1   (Hardback)
13 digit ISBN: 978 0 431 03252 8 (Hardback)
10 09 08 07 06
10 9 8 7 6 5 4 3 2 1

10 digit ISBN: 0 431 03259 9   (Paperback)
13 digit ISBN: 978 0 431 03259 7 (Paperback)
10 09 08 07 06
10 9 8 7 6 5 4 3 2 1

British Library Cataloguing in Publication Data
Clissold, Caroline
Investigating landscapes
91'.02
A full catalogue record for this book is available from the British Library.

Acknowledgements
The publishers would like to thank the following for permission to reproduce photographs:
Alamy Images p. **11** (The Photolibrary Wales), p. **27** (Davo Blair); Corbis Royalty Free p. **4, 6, 12**; Corbis p. **10** (WildCountry), p. **17** (Charles & Josette Lenars); Digital Vision p. **19**; Getty Images p. **29** (AFP); Grand Canyon National Park p. **13**; Ian Murray p. **20**; Oxford Scientific Films p. **23** (Nick Gordon); Photodisc pp. **5l, 5r, 15**; Rex Features p. **26** (Shout); Still Pictures p. **25** (Gordon Wiltsie), p. **28** (Nigel Dickinson); Topfoto p. **24** (Woodmansterne).

Cover photograph of a desert, reproduced with permission of Photolibrary.com.

The publishers would like to thank Rebecca Harman, Rachel Bowles, Robyn Hardyman, and Caroline Landon for their assistance in the preparation of this book.

Exploring further

Throughout this book you will find links to the Heinemann Explore CD-ROM and website at www.heinemannexplore.com. Follow the links to find out more about the topic.

Contents

Any words appearing in the text in bold, **like this**, are explained in the glossary.

What is a landscape?

In geography we study different **landscapes**. A landscape is the natural scenery we see around us like **mountains**, **deserts**, and forests. In our studies, we need to look at what these landscapes are, where they are, how they were formed, and what effect they have on our **environment**. Our environment is our physical surroundings.

Starting points

To find out about different landscapes you can look for pictures and information in geography books, **atlases**, and other reference books. Travel brochures and the Internet can also be useful.

How many different kinds of landscape do you think there are? In this book we will look at mountains, deserts, forests, and **polar** regions. What are these landscapes like? One of the features of a desert is a lack of rain. Can you think of some of the features of the other landscapes you know about?

■ A mountain landscape is made up of steep-sided mountains with valleys between them.

- A forest landcape is one that is covered in trees. These can be of several different types, as we will see later in this book.

- A desert landscape is very dry. It gets less than 250 millimetres (19.75 inches) of rain each year.

Activity

Think about your local area. These are some questions to ask about it:

1 What is the landscape like?

2 Are there any slopes? Do they make a hill or valley?

3 Where are there woodland and open grassy places?

4 Does a river play an important part in your area?

5 Can you go somewhere for a view of the landscape?

6 Are you near the sea?

Mountain landscapes

What is a mountain environment?

What is the difference between a **mountain** and a hill? Both are steep-sided areas of land, but what makes a mountain a mountain? A mountain is generally much higher and steeper than a hill. Mountain heights are measured in metres above sea level. In the UK a mountain is usually over 300 metres (1000 feet). It rises considerably above the surrounding land, often to a **peak** and always with steep sides. A hill is smaller and usually rounder.

■ *Mountains give the World some of its most amazing scenery. A very high mountain can look lush and green at its foot. It can be rocky and covered with snow at its peak.*

Where are mountain environments found?

Mountains can be found all over the world in many different places. Sometimes single peaks and **ridges** poke out of the flat ground. Sometimes single mountains rise from the sea. Most mountains are found together in big groups called mountain **ranges**. Many mountain ranges are found on the edges of **continents**. Many mountain ranges join together to form mountain systems or chains. The biggest of these are the Himalayas, the Rocky Mountains, and the Andes.

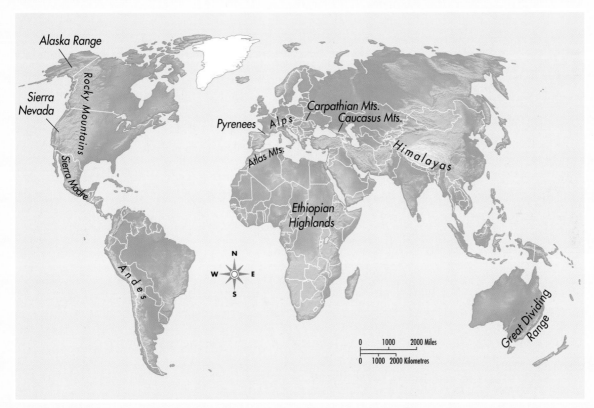

■ *This map shows mountain ranges around the world. The world's tallest mountain, Mount Everest, can be found in the Himalayas. It is a huge 8848 metres (29,000 feet) tall.*

Exploring further

On the Heinemann Explore website or CD-ROM click on Exploring > Mountains. Read the article 'Where in the world do we find mountains?' to find out more information about mountain ranges, single mountains, and underwater mountains. Then try doing the activity at the side of the article.

How are mountains formed?

The Earth's rocky outside layer is called its **crust**. This crust is made up of several huge slabs of moving rock called plates. Six or seven large plates now cover most of the Earth's surface. The plates move very slowly all the time. Below the crust, the rock that makes up the Earth is so hot that it has melted. We call molten rock **magma**. The plates move because the magma they are resting on is soft. Over millions of years, the movement of the plates makes the layers of rock fold, crack, and lift up to form **mountains**.

Types of mountain

Fold mountains

Fold mountains are formed when two tectonic plates move towards each other. Layers of rocks near the Earth's surface are scrunched together. Enormous forces buckle the rocks, folding them over to make mountains. Huge mountain ranges, like the Rockies and the Himalayas, are fold mountains. The Himalayas formed about 50 million years ago when India crashed into the rest of Asia!

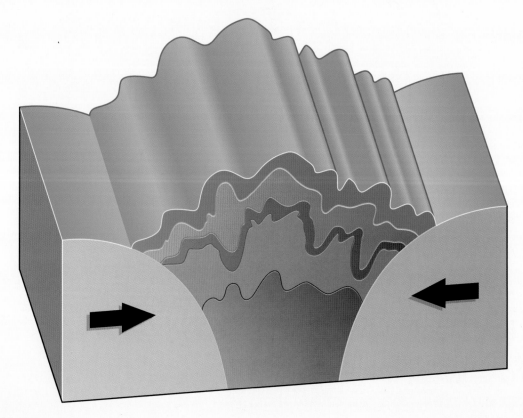

■ *Fold mountain*

Block mountains

Movement under the Earth's crust can create cracks called faults. This causes blocks of rock to slip up or down the faults, so that some blocks rise above the others. These are called block mountains. Mount Rundle in Banff National Park, Canada, is a good example of a block mountain.

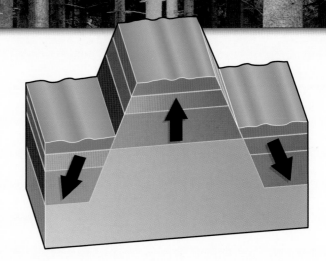

■ *Block mountains*

Dome mountains

In areas where the Earth's crust is thin or there is a weakness, magma can move upwards, pushing up the layers of rock above it. This forms a large bulge called a dome mountain. Many of the **peaks** in the Lake District in England are dome mountains.

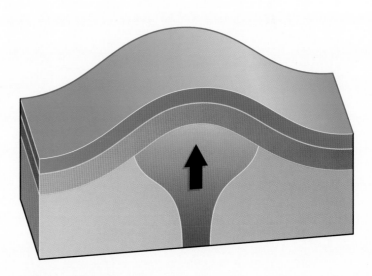

■ *Dome mountain*

Volcanoes

Volcanoes are mountains where magma leaks out through the Earth's crust. The magma is runny; it flows out of the hole in the crust and quickly cools to become solid. Volcanic mountains often have a **crater** in their **summit**. There are thousands of volcanoes in the world that we never see because they are hidden in the oceans. Some of them are the tallest mountains on Earth.

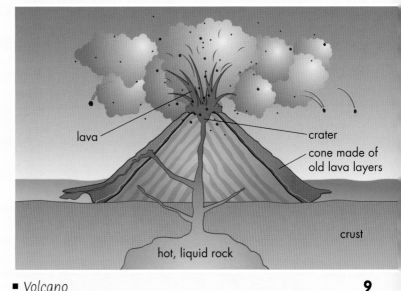

lava

crater

cone made of old lava layers

crust

hot, liquid rock

■ *Volcano*

Mountains in the UK

If you look at a map of the UK, you will see that **mountains**, especially those over 610 metres (2000 feet), are found in Scotland, Wales, and northern England. There are also a few mountains in Northern Ireland.

Scotland: the Grampians

The Grampians mountain **range** includes Ben Nevis, which is the highest mountain in the UK. It is 1343 metres (4406 feet) high. The Grampians are made of different types of rock, including granite, gneiss, quartzite, marble, and schist.

■ This map shows the mountain ranges of the UK.

■ Ben Nevis is the highest mountain in the UK.

Activity

Look at an Ordnance Survey (OS) map of the area around Ben Nevis. Find out the names of five rivers that have their sources there.

Wales: Snowdonia

Snowdonia is the mountainous region of North Wales. The tallest **peak** there is Mount Snowdon, which stands at a height of 1085 metres (3560 feet) above sea level. Some people like to climb it, but for others there is a railway that runs all the way to the **summit**. Snowdonia was made into a **National Park** in 1951. It is a popular **tourist** area for camping, walking, climbing, and horse riding.

■ *Mount Snowdon is the highest mountain in Wales.*

England: the Lake District and the Pennines

Often called hills and fells, there are many mountain peaks in these regions, especially ones over 600 metres (2000 feet). The Pennines are known as 'the backbone of England'. Their highest peak is Cross Fell, at 893 metres (2930 feet). In the Lake District, Scafell Pike reaches 978 metres (3209 feet) and Helvellyn, which is an easier climb, is 950 metres (3117 feet).

All mountainous areas have unpredictable weather conditions, even those in England. When walking or climbing in these areas, people need the correct footwear and clothes, and must take notice of **weather** forecasts.

The Rocky Mountains

The Rocky Mountains (the Rockies) are a long chain of **mountains** down the western side of North America. They are about 5300 kilometres (3300 miles) long. It stretches from the Mexican **plateau**, north through the west-central states of the USA and Canada, to the border with Alaska.

What kind of mountains are they?

The Rockies are folded mountains. They first started pushing upwards over 190 million years ago, and they are still rising today. Mount McKinley is the highest **peak** in the Rockies. At its highest point it is 6194 metres (20,320 feet) above sea level.

Landscape

The mountain chain has many different **landscapes**, from sharp peaks, like Mount McKinley, to the flat-topped rocks of the Grand Canyon. There has been a lot of **erosion** of the rocks over millions of years. There are wide valleys worn out by **glaciers** and deep **gorges** carved by rivers. There are also long ribbon-shaped lakes and hot volcanic springs. The sources of many rivers are found in the Rocky Mountains.

■ *Mount McKinley (also called Denali) is the highest mountain in North America.*

Land use

In the mountains there are many natural **resources**, including coal, oil, natural gas, copper, and gold. Many of these resources are mined and sold. **Lumbering** and cattle and sheep farming take place in the northern Rockies. There are also many **National Parks**, which attract lots of **tourists**.

Climate

The Rockies pass through many different **climate** zones, from the frozen lands of Alaska in the north, to hot and sunny Mexico in the south.

Life in the Rockies

The Rocky Mountains have a rugged **terrain**. This has made it impossible to develop the area, so the mountains have

■ *The Grand Canyon was carved out of the rocks by the Colorado River.*

a small **population**. Very small plants grow on the peaks of the mountains. Below these on the mountain-side are grasses and small shrubs, then huge forests and, down in the valleys, grassland slopes. The animals that live in the Rockies include deer, black bear, Rocky Mountain bighorn sheep, American elk, and coyote.

Exploring further

Go to the Heinemann Explore website or CD-ROM. Click on Exploring > Mountains, read the article 'The Rocky Mountains' to learn more about this mountain **range**, then complete the activity on the same page.

Desert landscapes

What is a desert landscape?

A **desert** is an **arid** region that gets less than 250 millimetres (19.75 inches) of rain in a year. This rainfall is usually very irregular – it may all fall in one month. Deserts have little or no **vegetation** as their soils are **infertile**. Desert surfaces are usually rocky or stony: only a small part is covered with loose sand.

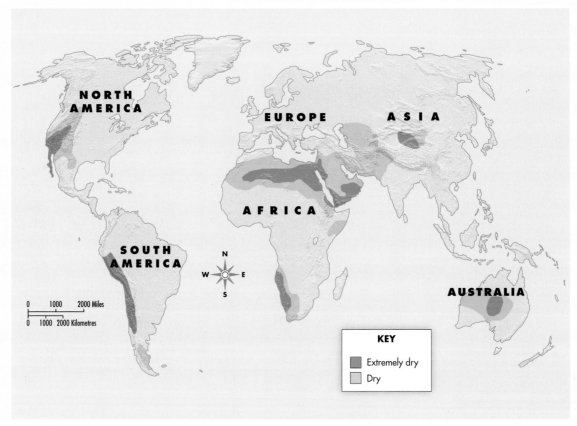

- *This map shows the location of the main deserts in the world.*

Types of desert

Deserts can be hot or cold. In **tropical** deserts (near the **equator**) the range in temperature during the day is extreme. Daytime temperatures can reach 58 °C (136.4 °F) and temperatures can fall well below freezing at night.

In deserts that are in the middle of **continents**, temperatures are much lower in the winter than in the summer. In the Gobi Desert in Mongolia, for example, the average temperature is below freezing for half the year.

Antarctica also counts as a desert because it is so dry. This freezing cold continent receives less than 50 millimetres (2 inches) of rain or snow in a year; some parts have had no rain for 2 million years.

Erosion in the desert

Although it does not rain very often in deserts, when it does, it pours down on the hard surfaces and wears them away. The rain collects in **rivulets** and wears **gullies** into the rocks. The rivulets meet each other at the bottom of rocky hills and combine to make rivers. These rivers start to carve out **canyons** or **gorges**. The canyons and gorges divide the land into high, flat areas called **plateaux**. The rivers dry up very quickly when it stops raining.

■ *These landforms were created by **erosion** of the desert landscape.*

Exploring further

Go to Resources > Deserts on the Heinemann Explore website or CD-ROM, watch the video on the Sahara Desert and make notes on what the landscape is like.

The Sahara Desert

The Sahara is the largest **desert** in the world. It covers an area of about 7 million square kilometres (2.7 million square miles).

■ *The Sahara Desert is in the north of Africa. It stretches from the Atlantic Ocean in the west, to the Red Sea in the east.*

Landscape

The Sahara Desert is mainly a rocky **plateau**, with a central **mountain range**. About one-fifth of the desert is made up of seas of sand.

Land use

At one time, salt was one of the desert's most precious **resources**. It was traded with Europe. Salt is still carried by camels from the salt mines to Timbuktu in Mali to the south. **Mineral** resources, such as iron ore, are still found in Algeria and Mauritania, and **phosphates** are found in Morocco and the western Sahara.

Climate

The central areas of the desert have the highest temperatures in all of Africa. Afternoon temperatures in summer can be more than 44 °C (111 °F). In winter the average temperature is below 15 °C (59 °F) and frosts are not unusual. The amount of rainfall varies across the Sahara. The very **arid** centre gets less than 50 millimetres (2 inches) per year – in the UK we often get that much rain each month!

Life in the Sahara

The Tuareg people are **nomads** who traditionally live in the Sahara Desert. They are great traders who use camels to transport high-quality, high-value goods such as jewellery and leather. The Tuareg people roam the desert looking for water. They make their homes in tents around **oases**.

■ *The Tuareg people breed animals, such as camels, cows, goats, and sheep. Their animals provide them with milk, cheese, meat, and transportation, so are very important to them.*

There is not much plant and animal life in the Sahara, as most plants and animals need lots of water to live. Dates and other fruits grow around the wells of the oases. Some animals, such as gazelles, hyenas, jackals, antelopes, and foxes, live in the desert.

Activity

Find out as much as you can about the life of the Tuareg people. You will need to use an **atlas**, reference books, travel guides, and the Internet. Try to find out:

1 How they cope with the weather.
2 What their homes are like.
3 What they eat.

Polar landscapes

What is a polar landscape?

The **polar** regions are large areas of extreme cold. They cover about 15 per cent of the world's surface, and much of this area is ice. There are two polar regions: the Arctic in the north and the Antarctic in the south.

The Arctic

The Arctic is the region between the Arctic Circle (**latitude** 66 °N) and the North Pole. This area includes the Arctic Ocean and the northernmost parts of North America, Europe, and Asia. There is a large **ice sheet** covering Greenland, and the Arctic Ocean freezes over in winter.

■ *This map shows the area of the Arctic.*

The Antarctic

The region between the Antarctic Circle (latitude 66°S) and the South Pole includes the **continent** of Antarctica. Antarctica is almost totally covered in ice, and floating **icebergs** cover the seas around the land. The highest point in Antarctica is Vinson Massif, which is 5140 metres (16,863 feet) above sea level.

■ *Animal life on Antarctica includes whales, seals, emperor penguins, king penguins, and 67 different types of insects.*

What is the weather like?

The **weather** in polar regions is extremely cold and dry. In summer, the central areas of the polar regions are in complete daylight, all day, every day. In winter they are in total darkness, all day, every day.

Even in summer, the temperatures in the polar regions are still very cool. Very few of the Sun's rays hit the land, so the region hardly warms up. The rays that do hit the land are reflected back towards the Sun by the white ice. In the winter it is always dark so there are no light rays from the Sun and it is freezing cold all the time.

In Antarctica, winter temperatures can fall as low as −89 °C (−128 °F). The ocean warms the Arctic, so temperatures here are warmer than in the Antarctic. Arctic winter temperatures only fall to −34 °C (−30 °F) and in the summer, temperatures can rise to 0 °C. This rise in temperature causes parts of the floating ice to melt.

Exploring further

To learn more about polar regions go to the Heinemann Explore website or CD-ROM. In Exploring > Polar regions, click on the article 'All about Greenland' to discover what life is like for the people living there.

Forest landscapes

What is a forest landscape?

Forests are very important to our **environment**. They provide us with **resources**, such as food, timber, and medicines. Forests are home to more than half of the world's plants and animals.

Types of forest

Temperate forests grow in places where the temperatures are not extreme. The main types of trees in these forests are **broadleaved trees**, such as oak, beech, and elm. These trees are deciduous, which means they lose their leaves each winter.

Tropical forests are found along the **equator**, where it is hot and humid all year round. Temperatures here range from 20 °C. to 28 °C. It rains in these forests almost every day.

Boreal forests are the coldest, driest forests in the world. Temperatures are always very low, sometimes falling to −70 °C in the winter. The winters are very long, but the summers are warm enough for plants to grow.

■ *Temperate forests are found in the UK where the summers are warm, the winters are cool, and there is a steady amount of rainfall each year.*

Where are forests found?

Tropical forests grow near the equator in South America, Africa and southern Asia. The world's largest tropical rainforest is the Amazon in Brazil, South America. It covers an area of 6 million square kilometres (2,316,600 square miles).

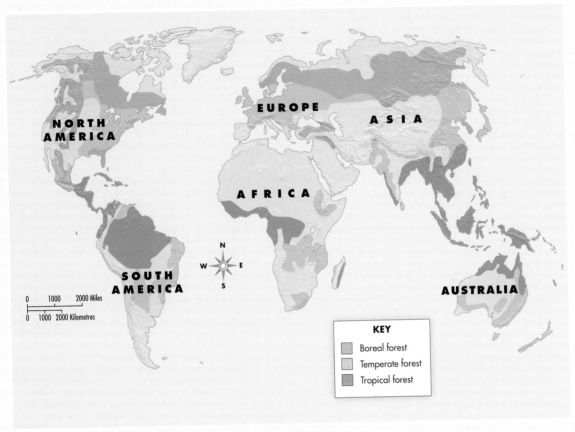

■ *This map shows where each type of forest can be found.*

Boreal forests are found in the northern hemisphere, covering areas of North America, northern Asia and northern Europe. The largest areas of boreal forest are in Russia and Canada.

Temperate forests grow in areas between the tropical forests and the boreal forests. They are found mostly in the northern hemisphere in Europe, North America, and central Asia. The tallest trees in the world grow along the west coast of the USA. They are giant **conifers** called sequoias. The tallest sequoia is over 95 metres (312 feet) tall.

Amazon tropical rainforest

Tropical rainforests grow near the **equator** in South America, Africa and southern Asia, where the climate is hot and wet. Temperatures are usually 20–28 °C. It rains almost every day and there are usually thunderstorms in the afternoons.

Plant life

A huge variety of plant life grows in tropical rainforests. There are usually four layers of plants, all fighting to get to the light:

- The forest floor is the lowest layer. It gets little sunlight so it is dark and gloomy. The floor is covered with mosses, **fungi**, ferns, and rotten leaves.
- The understorey is the next layer, from the forest floor up to about 20 metres (66 feet). Small trees, such as palms and young trees, sprout up in the gaps on the forest floor.
- The canopy is above the understorey, from about 20 metres (66 feet) up to 40 metres (131 feet). The canopy is a mass of treetops that form a roof over the forest floor and trap warm air and most of the water from the rain.
- The emergent layer is the highest layer, from about 40 metres (131 feet) up to 60 metres (197 feet). A few very tall trees have their tops here.

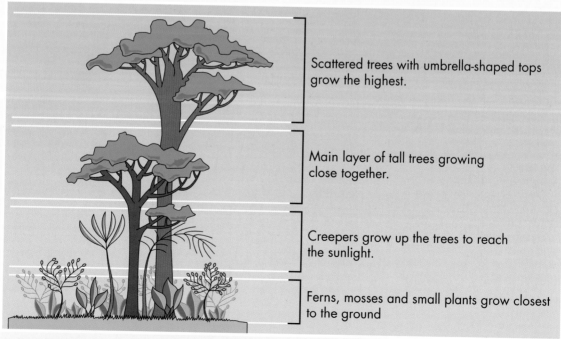

Scattered trees with umbrella-shaped tops grow the highest.

Main layer of tall trees growing close together.

Creepers grow up the trees to reach the sunlight.

Ferns, mosses and small plants grow closest to the ground

■ *These are the different layers of the tropical rainforest.*

Animal life

On the forest floor you can see animals, such as coatis and capybaras, which have long snouts for searching out grubs and insects. The understorey is home to lizards, anteaters, and tarantulas. The canopy is full of life. Creatures such as toucans, sloths, parrots, woolly monkeys, snakes, and macaws live here. The emergent layer is home to spider and howler monkeys, opossums, hummingbirds, and iguanas. Howler monkeys are the noisiest animals in the tropical forest.

People of the forest

The Yanomami people live in the Amazon rainforest. They build huge circular houses called yanos, and twenty families share one yano. Outside their homes, the Yanomami clear small patches of forest to grow maize, sweet potatoes, bananas, and cassava. They use this farm for two or three years, then leave it to grow back into forest.

■ *The Yanomami people live in the Amazon rainforest in Brazil, South America.*

Exploring further

Watch the video about the tropical rainforest on the Heinemann Explore website or CD-ROM. Think about what it would be like to live in this kind of environment.

How is the weather different in different landscapes

Mountain landscapes

Mountains are found in many different places all over the world, from the frozen mountains of Alaska to the hot mountains of the **deserts**. At the base of a mountain, the temperature is the same as in the surrounding region. Higher up the mountain, the temperature starts to fall. It can be extremely cold at the top of the highest mountains. Many have snow on them all year round.

- *It often rains in the mountains. These are in Glencoe, Scotland.*

Mountains are usually rainy, especially if one side faces the sea. The wind blows rain clouds from the sea on to the land. When they meet a mountain, the rain clouds rise up and drop their rain. On the other side of the mountain it is dry. This is called a **rain shadow** area. You often find deserts in these areas.

Activity

Tibet is a country in Asia that is hidden on three sides by mountains.

1 Find Tibet in your **atlas**.
2 Think about the **weather** in mountain **environments**. How do you think the weather conditions might affect life in Tibet?

Desert landscapes

Deserts can be hot or cold, or even both. The one thing that all deserts have in common is that they get less than 250 millimetres (19.75 inches) of rain in a year.

Tropical deserts have the same weather conditions throughout the year. In other deserts the weather is more seasonal; there are still hot days and cold nights, but these are of a higher temperature in the summer than in the winter. In **polar** deserts, such as Antarctica, it is extremely cold all year round.

Polar landscapes

In polar regions in summer, the temperature increases a little and some of the ice melts. The hours of daylight increase as well. In the winter, it is dark most of the time and the temperature is well below freezing, down to −60 °C in the Antarctic. When it is this cold there is very little rain or snow.

Tropical rainforests

Tropical rainforests are hot, wet, and humid all year round. It rains almost every day and there are frequent thunderstorms.

Activity

Note down all the weather words you associate with:

1 Mountains
2 Deserts
3 Polar regions
4 Tropical rainforests.

■ *Do you think you could cope with being outside in temperatures this low?*

What effect does the weather in different landscapes have on tourism?

Why do people go away on holiday? Think about where your family goes on holiday and why. Is the **weather** important to your choice? Does the weather affect where you go on holiday? The answer is probably yes. You might want it to be hot so you can swim in the sea. If you want there to be snow so that you can go skiing, you would visit a **mountain** landscape.

The weather of a landscape plays a big part in whether it becomes popular with **tourists**.

Tourism in mountain landscapes

Mountains are very popular areas for tourists to visit. As the weather is cold in winter, snow can lie on the ground for a long time. This makes these regions ideal for skiing and snowboarding holidays. When the snow melts in summer hikers visit the area, either climbing up the mountains or walking in the valleys below.

▪ *On dry days it is possible to go hiking in mountain landscapes. These people are walking in an Alpine valley in Switzerland*

Tourism in desert landscapes

It is possible to go on jeep **safaris,** and climbing and hiking in some of the more accessible **deserts**, such as the Negev Desert in Israel. In some areas, such as in Sinai, Egypt, there are beaches next to deserts. Many people also visit the pyramids in the desert. The temperature is extreme and the landscape harsh in desert regions. Visitors must be careful to cover up and wear lots of sun cream to protect themselves.

■ *These tourists are in Yosemite National Park.*

Tourism in forest landscapes

There are few tourists in **tropical** forests or **boreal** forests, as the weather is too extreme and the landscape too dangerous, but **temperate** forests are visited by many people. Think about your local forest or woods. People enjoy walking in them and looking at the wildlife. In the temperate forests of the western USA, tourists come in huge numbers to see the enormous sequoia trees.

Tourism in polar landscapes

The polar regions do not attract as many tourists as other areas, because of their cold temperatures and difficult **terrain**. But visitors are starting to go to these areas as people search for more unusual places to visit

Activity

1 Look in a travel brochure to find a holiday destination in a desert landscape and one in a mountain landscape.

2 How would the weather affect what you would do on holiday in each place?

What effect does tourism have on different landscapes?

People travel to different areas and countries for many different reasons, and some places are more popular than others. **Tourism** can have a big effect on a place. These effects may be good or bad for the country.

Mountain and forest landscapes

Many of the **mountainous** countries in the Himalayan region, such as Nepal, India, Pakistan, Bhutan, China, and Myanmar, have encouraged tourism in the mountains. The increased number of people visiting the region means that more fuel is needed for cooking, more wood is needed for building hotels, and more land is needed for growing food. This results in large areas of forest **landscape** being cut down to supply the wood and make way for roads and hotels. When forests are cut down, it leads to more soil **erosion**, which can result in **landslides**.

■ Clearing forests to make way for roads and hotels can have a bad effect on the landscape.

Mount Everest Base Camp

As the scale of tourism increases, the effects on the landscape increase, as is shown by the problem of rubbish at the Base Camp of Mount Everest in the Himalayas, Nepal. Mount Everest is the highest mountain in the world, and for this reason Everest Base Camp is a popular destination for trekking holidays. This has some advantages for the local people, as they can earn money by carrying rucksacks for the tourists and providing food for them. However, the tourists also leave their rubbish at the Base Camp. This has a devastating effect on the landscape of this beautiful area.

Some local people have realized that tourists will no longer come to their area if the landcape is ruined. They have set up a project called the Sagarmatha Pollution Control Project in the Everest Base Camp area. They burn most of the rubbish and remove anything that cannot be burned.

■ Some of the many oxygen canisters left behind by mountaineers who have climbed Mount Everest.

Glossary

atlas book of maps

arid very dry

boreal the coldest, driest forests of the world

butte pointed rock that stands alone in the desert, as the rest of the land has been eroded away

broad leaved tree tree that loses its leaves in autumn and grows new ones in spring. Another name for a broadleaved tree is deciduous.

canyon deep valley carved out of rock by a river

climate the average weather conditions in a place over a period of time

conifer cone-bearing tree with needles

continent one of the main masses of land in the world

crater bowl-shaped hole in the land or in the top of a volcano

crust the layer of solid rock that forms the outer layer of the Earth

desert large area of very dry, often sandy land

environment natural and man-made things that make up our surroundings

equator imaginary line running round the Earth at its widest point

erosion wearing away of rocks and soil by wind, water, or ice

fungi simple plants, such as mould, mushrooms, or toadstools

glacier slow moving river of ice

gorge deep valley carved out of rock by a river

gully narrow channel in rock

iceberg large chunk of floating ice that has broken off a glacier and fallen into the sea

ice sheet very thick layer of ice that covers a large area of land

infertile too poor in quality for plants to grow

landscape scenery and its features

landslide when a large amount of soil and rock falls down the side of a mountain

latitude distance north or south from the Equator

lumbering cutting down trees to sell their wood

magma very hot liquid rock that lies below the Earth's surface

mineral hard substance that can be dug out of the ground, such as coal

mountain landform that rises at least 300 metres (1000 feet) above sea level

National Park area of landscape that is protected because of its natural beauty

nomad person who moves from place to place hunting, gathering food, or feeding animals

oasis place in a desert where water is found

peak top of a mountain

phosphate substance made from the chemical element phosphorus

plateau area of high, flat land

polar   the areas around the North and South Poles at the top and bottom of the Earth

population   the number of people living in a place

rain shadow   dry side of a mountain because the clouds have shed all their rain on the other side

range   a group of mountains formed at the same time and in the same way

resource   something that humans can use, such as salt, coal, oil, natural gas, copper, and gold

ridge   long, narrow peak or range of mountains

rivulet   small channel formed by running water

safari   journey, especially to see wild animals

summit   top of a mountain or volcano

temperate   region of the world where the temperatures are not extreme and rainfall is steady throughout the year

terrain   landscape of an area

tourist   person who visits a place for pleasure

tropical   region of the world near the equator

vegetation   plants

weather   rain, snow, sunshine, cloud, and wind at a particular time or place

Find out more

Books

Landscapes and people: Earth's changing mountains, Neil Morris (Raintree, 2004).

Landscapes and people: Earth's changing deserts, Neil Morris (Raintree, 2004).

Website

www.heinemannexplore.com

Discover much more about the different landscapes studied in this book by visiting the landscapes section of the Heinemann Explore Geography website. Along with lots of extra information, you will find videos, animations, and activities.

Index

Titles in the *Explore Geography* series include:

Hardback   0 431 03293 9

Hardback   0 431 03254 8

Hardback   0 431 03257 2

Hardback   0 431 03252 1

Hardback   0 431 03251 3

Hardback   0 431 03253 X

Hardback   0 431 03256 4

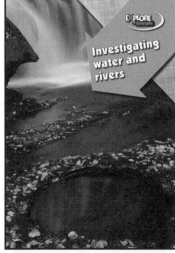

Hardback   0 431 03255 6

Find out about other titles from Heinemann Library on our website www.heinemann.co.uk/library